Sweet Smiles & Tender Thoughts

Mary Winnifred Fraser

PublishAmerica
Baltimore

ISBN: 1-4241-1209-5
PUBLISHED BY PUBLISHAMERICA, LLLP
www.publishamerica.com
Baltimore

Printed in the United States of America

Dedications

This book is dedicated with love to my children, Bill and Elizabeth; who have given me great material to write about.

My granddaughter, Shaughnessy. (my little shining star) who always makes my world just right.

To Don who always believes in me and stands behind and beside me 100% of the way, in my venture to become a writer.

My friend and mentor, Darrel Day; who has encouraged me from the very start to challenge myself and has believed in me all the way.

Without Darrel's' honest feedback and support; this book would be still a childhood dream of a seven year old.

I love each and every one of you with all my heart.

Mary Winnifred Fraser

Just Be You… But Take Notes

To all those who teach by allowing us to read.

So many creative minds out here;
could put you in a block.
An opinion, review or tear shed for someone there.
Could make me take a walk.

I have read such beauty,
Cried for hours; as I read the tearful words, heart tugging
pleas.
Of war, starvation, depravation; plus the lack of men in
powers.

Oh I am no spineless chicken here,
just a newbie in this forum.
Read my words…with thoughtful eyes
there is a message in subtle disguise.

Your gifts of words go with value and trust;
Flower it up…
That's' not me…
For if I did…it would be a bust.

Whispering Words of Willow Trees

That's not me you see.
I write from my heart…
Straight out and true.
Honest, loving, gentle, truthful to be sure.

The humbleness of reading your words;
Brings me to my knees.
I feel joy; remorse; pity; resounding memories record;
as I lay blue eyes upon this screen; my heart held in my
hand.

You captured my essence of living;
you showered my life with joy;
you have dropped me to my knees with forgiving.
This forum is not a toy.

WE write for many reasons;
of which I know a few.
Once a change of seasons.
Now it is…to grow anew.

To be re-born with wisdom
isn't…what all do have.
To be born with a cherished mind.
Is a gift from God above.

Savor each word…spice it up.
Learn from your mentors.
Take notes…write it up!
NEVER defer from the real YOU!
Or you will have dandelions for your sup.

Poems of Inspiration

Whispers of Angels

As our body lays down to sleep,
Silent whispers tend to keep;
Watching over all of their flock;
Patient as the never-ending; tick of a clock.
A gentle fluttering of wings;
Do guide us as we sleep.
Your angel whispers to mine…
The victories and stresses of the day;
Watching over us even as we play.
Tiny little angels; creatures great or small.
Whisper to God; how loved we are.
Your angel tells mine how you fare.
Mine does the same in a whispered tone.
Holding a gentle touch over us; on this land.
Go forth…rest well; for they will keep,
Us safe and sound as we lay down to sleep.
Loving whispers do go round and round.
Blessing us; far from above.
Surround us with God's sweet love.

Heaven Bed

Shhhhh don't make a sound,
The wee one still sleeps.
In one tiny second; she will fully rebound;
Asking a million questions, as she dances on tiny feet.
"Where do we go from here?" she will question.
An answer is a must…being indifferent won't quench her
thirst.
"Shall we go see Auntie, Momma?" she will ask with a
sigh.
Five years old; she knows her Auntie is very sick.
"Yes baby," you reply "but please stay quiet."
"Of course Momma; I will speak very soft to Auntie"
Suddenly out of the blue, the child did speak once again.
"Momma," she said with a painful sound.
"Is Auntie going to be in her Heaven Bed soon?'
Taking a deep agonizing breath; the little girls' Momma,
slightly smiled;
Looked at her child, her eyes wide open knowing the
answer.
"It's ok Momma?" God needs us all but not all of us
today.
"Auntie, will have a special place;
I will put a picture in her Heaven Bed for God to remember,
So all of her friends can come and play.
The sound of the child made the saying of goodbye,
Less of a reason to sit and cry.
She is so certain that each of us has a Heaven Bed,
I know she is an Earthly Angel; to ease our pain.

D. Day… Your Pain is Mine
as Well

D. popped in to say hello today.
Asked how my night had been; with no concern for him.
Right I said with fumbling fingers; typos a plenty too.
Rest your hands he said; you will hurt yourself D. did say.
Each of your pinkies is making a mess
Lay your head down; time to take some rest.

DARREL; read between the lines my friend.
All you have ever asked is "How is your day going hun?
Yes you are a special one, full of love, respect; a gift of love to mankind.
I applaud the day you became my friend.

Laugh and chuckle with me anytime.
Of course you know how I adore you; please share your pain with me?
Victories will soon come your way.
Enough to make your head and heart feel as one

You know in my prayers you are each night.
Our Lord does hear let alone,
Understands D's daily fight.

God has spoken;
Open your heart, mind, spirit and soul.
Don't let D. down; open your heart to understanding;
learn how to survive.
I Pray...
Will You Join With Me?
Dear Lord I beg of You;
one more boon today.
Please allow Your son D. to have sweet joyous days.
Chase away the terror that rips;
his heart and mind to shreds.
Erase I beg...
Our Heavenly Father...
D.s dreaded bi-polar illness.
Tis a burden he carries
Many hearts fill with tears.
Not tears of self pity...
I know D. better than that My Lord.
Darrel has your need.
Listen to my heart My Lord;
Your Son D.; is in need of your gentle touch.
Wrap your tender, loving, healing arms around D.s'
heart and soul.
Please let D. feel your healing hug.
Please Bless Darrel...
Allow this illness to leave his space.
Our Blessed Father;
Hear my heart crying out loud.
Erase D.'s illness,
Allow D, to learn how to win and survive.

Coping with bi-polar depression
Leaves Your Son; with too much pain,
It fogs his thought process;
Condemns his spirit with,
A permanent fear of NO GAIN.
Yes My Lord, My Savior;
You graced D. with talent to share;
The horrors he and others suffer.
Will educate others that…I know.
I beg of You Sweet Jesus
Make D. laugh with your complete, honest loving gift.
D. does offer all he has to others asking nothing in return.
We need to help D. and those who suffer bi-polar depression.
Please heal my friend.
Your son has helped so many; while in his own torment.
Darrel; Offers all of us 100%.
Tis time to make amends.
Teach me Dear Jesus; how to ease D's pain.
Amen

Kylie Champa Has Need of Prayer

To Kylie Champa with love .Be tough little one.

Today I heard of a child in pain,
suffering with a cancerous disease.
Kylie I know your fears this day.
I pray in Our Lords' Name.

Dear Jesus please hear our pleas;
allow Kylie a cure from this dreaded disease.
Kylie is just twelve years old.
A child in all who's heart has a special hold.
Grant us one special wish.
Show Kylie your Spirit to behold.
The fight is a rough and rocky road.
Carrying such a heavy load;
Does tear our hearts in many pieces.
I ask of You my Sweet Gentle Lord.
Please hear our prayers.
Allow Kylie the strength to fight.
Keep her sweet smile in your sight.
Offer Kylie and her family,
to know love and prayers come from ever so many.
Guide Kylies' family with love.
Offer them strength from Your Love Above.
Surround this child with angels a plenty.
Show our true love in each starry night.
Guide this child in your hearts pure light.
Kylie be strong,
know you are never alone.

Our love is with you;
you face this fight not alone.
We all are with your in this fight.
Please Dear Jesus; show us your light.
This twelve year old has much wisdom;
We are on bended knee pleading for intervention.
Bless sweet Kylie as she sleeps,
As she fights.
Cure her pain I ask with devotion.
God bless you Kylie and your parents.
Your last name tells the story of your true worth.
Champa...you are a wonderful one at that.
I'll carry your name in my heart each night.

God bless you and yours always.

Share What Little I Have

I suppose there isn't much I can do
except share what little I have.

This world is mighty empty,
hearts are filled with woes.
Most talk about the weather,
instead of how others' lives do go.
Look at the starving children
mothering instincts takes over.
Bring all the little children
my loving arms will keep.

I suppose there isn't much I can do
except share what little I have.

Offer starving people
food to feed those at hand.
Offer from our coffers
expertise in medicine.
Don't let disease and famine
destroy another solitary land.
Don't neglect to read the news
search for valued souls.

I suppose there isn't much I can do
except share what little I have.

Pray the droughts do sweep away
gentle rain assist; to plant crops at hand.
Show the struggles of mankind
on more than C.N.N.
Look into the children's' eyes
all across this world.
Share our words of grace
feed the hungry; love never to be erased.

I suppose there isn't much that I can do
except share what little I have.

Yes I do pray that all will survive
it is the greatest of my pleas.
I offer whatever dollars
my wallet will share with ease
Yes I too am a selfish onetaking care of my own.
When the day does come
I no longer have need of me.
Take whatever there is need of
this is my wish; do it; please!

I suppose there isn't much I can do
except share what little I have.

Shall we gain together
in one united force?
Pray for each other
God does love us so.
Share of your worldly goods
the extras you have at hand.
Don't forget the lost hungry child
could be the one next door; or in a far distant land.

I suppose there isn't much I can do
except share what little I have.

Shall we join a united front
teach each other's of each ones needs.
Stop the world of famine
bread and milk do ease.
Share the wealth we all have some
God's Blessings If You Please!
Stop disease that wipes out life
takes a loving families trust.

I suppose there isn't much I can do
except share what little I have.

Take my hand…would you please?
Join as one, a united front.
Make this world a better place
we are in this life called the human race.
We were created in His image
step forward to share as never before.
Your faith in God's sweet face
He gave His life, for us to share this hungry space.
I suppose there isn't much that I can do
except share what little I have.

What is a Goal?

Something you set out to do—
for today, for tomorrow.
Long-term desires—
gently stoking fires.
Keeping peace—
in all those I love.
Generating interest—
within the outside world.
Keeping an open mind—
in all that is around.
Determine what is real—
exactly how it feels.
Planning for tomorrow—
nothing grandiose.
Being realistic—
in my expectations.
Of myself and especially of others—
expect nothing; anticipate everything.
Never be surprised—
we are all unique.
Always laugh—
each and every day.
Touch someone with your smile—
a kind word goes a long, long way!
Feel for others—
their life is more troubled that mine.
As I am in control—
I know what has to be done.

Look into the mirror—
at the end of every day.
Knowing—
today's goal has been won.

A Halo From Above

A sweet young man lays lucky to be alive.
Went to a pub for a pint or two.
On his way home…jumped by a slug or two.
Found in the morning; near a graveyard.
Can't remember what happened; let alone who dared!
Thank God he is alive.
Innocent he was…keys in his hands.
A halo on his head; six weeks flat on his back in bed.
Now to forgive the evil one; who left this everlasting scar.
Tiss the season to forgive and forget.
Our heart is trying…spirit torn to commit.
I will say one day my brother will be whole.
Attackers' live with this; your punishment will be;
Sitting down by Our Lords' knee…as you begin to plea.
I forgive you today; tomorrow as well.
May your conscience support, last nights'…living hell!

We Are the Poets

We laugh, pray; rejoice in God's Heavenly Name.
Pray for one another in all moments of pain.
The power of His wondrous word.
Allows our hearts, beating, speaking; to be heard.

No More Blurry Eyes

I shall sleep when my eyes are too weary.
My head will nod; my eyes certainly are blurry.
As dawn approaches my thoughts written down.
Saved to memory as I quickly scurry round.
Another ditty certainly was born.
Without thought or process; my fingers take over.
Did I master each of my days' needs dreams and desires?
To make the transition of sadness to smiles.
Yes I can say without any doubt.
Caring of others is a joy I am proud of.
The time is coming as birds do awake.
Rejoicing in the rising moments of Heavens' Gate.
As they chirp and sing away.
I now know it is time to pray.
I am thankful for the day gone by.
Confident, in my rest; I shall not wonder why.
All sleepy thoughts fly out of my head.
Knowing my trust in You is wonderfully led.
Soon; I will be asleep; no more blurry eyes.
Happiness radiates from Heavenly skies.

Please Dear Jesus

Help find Cynthia Grey.

Please Dear Jesus hear our plea
I bow before you on bended knee
Pray to you with all my might
Please give us an answer
Make us strong each night
If I were a star high in the sky
I could answer your fears of where and why
Cynthia Ann Gray has gone missing for many a day.
Dear Jesus hear our cry
Please allow our hearts to start beating
Please stop our eyes from tearing
Please Dear Jesus
We beg of You
Show us your mercy
We know of Your love
Send word with your angels
Ease our heart and souls
Take away the confusion
Dear Jesus hear our cry
Word of our Cynthia Ann Grey
Would bless our day
Be it the words we want to hear
Or our worst felt fear
Please Dear Jesus
Send an answer
Allow our hearts to clear
Permit our fears to be answered

Mystery solved by your love
We bow down on bended knee
Please Dear Jesus
Pease hear our plea.
Show us how to find our way
to assist the family of
Cynthia Ann Grey
Amen

What If Today Was the Day?

What would you do if today was the day
you heard your first-born cry?
I kiss my babe and say; God blessed me today.

What would you do if today was the day
you lost your job?
I would cry out in pain then humbly pray.

What would you do if today was the day
your child left home for good?
I would say Please God; don't let him stray.

What would you do if today was the day
you lost your memory and was missing for days?
I would stumble and wander until God showed me the way.

What would you say if today was the day
a terrorist strikes out against your country?
I'd say dear Jesus; forgive them; hear us pray.

What would you do if today was the day
the world turned black with molten ash?
I would offer my help to all and pray.

What would you do if today was the day
all mankind was treated with love and respect?
I'd fall to my knees rejoicing and pray.

What would you do if today was the day
Our Lord took you home to stay?
I would say; Dear Jesus I have been ready for many a day.

One Mile

My goal set out many years ago.

The days of life run together.Tis up to me to make it
better.
I awake with a smile!
Another chance to walk one mile.
Not physically…but in every sense.
Reach out…touch someone.
A kind word and touch are common place.
In my world it is one of grace.
Be positive!
It takes me further.
Take the negative…turn it around.
Capture each moment; rewards do rebound.
I find serenity and peace.
Joy in my place.
Each day is a joy.
My sunrise to see.
Water surrounds; the air so clean.
Contentment set is, my spirit is found.
Where is your spirit?
It glows from within.
Greet each day with a smile.
You will find strength to go the extra mile.

Jesus Hear My Prayer

Jesus I ask of you to bless Encourager and her Mother;
In this; their time of need.
Her Mother is very ill.
I beg of…You my Mighty Lord;
Lay your loving tender hands upon their hearts;
To touch their soul.
Please my Father; send a message of pure love,
Guide us all in Prayer to You;
With Your Mighty Power
Allow Encourager and her family;
To have many years of Your love shining down;
From above and within our spirit.
Knowing the Power of your love.
Please heal Encouragers' Mom…
I beg of you.
My Dearest Savior I ask this of you…
To allow the glory of your might.
You give us unconditional love…For this I adore your
very presence in my life.
I bow down with prayer…
To allow; Encouragers', Mom,
The benefit of a long, spiritual, wondrous life.
Bless you, all of your sheep,
As we continue to pray for one another.
All in Your Name.
Amen

Sunshine

Awake I finally have become;
To see the glorious morning sun.
What angelic dreams did you have?
None…you see; I do not dream.
Sunshine on my face is a wondrous state.
It cleanses away all strife and pain.
My life is rich…I almost forgot;
Laughing voices on the phone; forget—me—not.
I am rich beyond my wildest wishes.
Now to just get up…do the dishes.
Out of my slump, I have finally risen.
May this be the last crash and burn;
Till the next one…then I'll take yet, another turn.

Bring on the sun!
I am ready to run!
Living is number one!

Teach Me

We start from a seed.
Our hearts do bleed.
When pain does start…
Remember; that is why…we have a heart.
To feel the need;
Not one of greed.
One of love.
Cradled; gently, from above.
I God's sweet hands; On our feet, we do land.
Often with a bounce along the way.
Close your eyes; open your hearts; pray.
Keep me strong.
Please…don't let me do wrong.
Teach me to love,
Blessed be your power…from above.

Help Is on Its Way

The winds do blow, fearsome and fearless.
People scatter; lives in tatters.
One slam after another.
Punch-drunk; from another onslaught.
Yet…much more is yet to come.
Which way to turn; no escape.
Head north, south, east, or west?
Flip a coin…all is a mess.
Hurricanes gather in force.
Island after island is devastated.
Everything; torn up-side down…
Waiting for another; onslaught.
How much more…can they take?
How strong a people; withstanding such a loss.
I pray for you…your safety.
I pray for food, water…necessities of life.
Medicine to halt disease; before it spreads;
to reach you and your loved ones; fast!
BE STRONG, STAY SAFE…HELP IS ON ITS' WAY!
My heart does bleed for your pain.
May God guide you…to safety…AGAIN!

Prayer for a Child

Starlight star bright
Watch over me tonight.
I pray to God to guide me.
Show me love, hope and joy,
Most of all...the gift of giving.
Not one of lies,
Nor one of greed or selfish living.One of honesty,
Truth and giving,
Of myself...
My joy and spirit.
Shine high in the sky.
As the Heavens...so bright.

One Tiny Question

How do I say; I won't take you for granted?
Would…thank you be enough?
I highly doubt it;
Like you…there are so few.
Does one tiny question have so much meaning?
Only one star has ever been so bright?
Are feelings of gratitude ever spoken?
Oh yes! Over and over, many times done,
What is so special you ask of me?
Your generous donation…
Giving life back…now he comes to me.
Without your spirit; as well your beliefs,
He would have passed away.
Your gift left a precious legacy to us.
Made it possible to live, love, laugh and be free.
We shall care for you; as you become one.
Your gift of life; WILL be present; from sunlight to
sundown.
Long, long ago you gave your liver to him.
We cherish your loving gesture;
With every fiber of our being.
Need we ask;
Would thank you be anywhere near enough?
The word is small but our hearts are full;
Of the debt of gratitude we owe to you.
God bless your loving family; all the days of their life.
Your gift has given me the chance to be his wife.
Thank you ever so much.

I Am

Final thoughts roll through my head
Sleep can wait; I write before bed.
If all I think of is writing,
waking to doodle a ditty,
Instead of resting my head.
Low and behold; some are meant to be read.
Who needs to sleep?
When my mind won't still.
Doodle away I say to myself.
One page after another gathers in piles.
Some create a glorious smile.
A few have been due to unwanted tears.
Most are due to, my youthful years.
I need to write to speak words unheard.
No voice is needed to break this dawn.
Now is my time of life, to write, as I need.
Read if you please...One once said,
"If all you think about is writing.
Then you must be a writer."
So I guess; I am!

Crash and Burn

Don't shake tonight I beg of you.
The ole hands can't do what the use to do.

My misery comes out in my fingers' touch.
Post—polio has spoiled my lunch.

This isn't the plan I had on sharing you.
Go ahead and mess with my head, eyes are blurry too.

WE had a deal you and I-do you need to see?
Some days I handle you; others you do me.

I can't crash and burn now I fear.
I have much to do myself; my dear.

I thought we could be friends for life.
Now you rear your head; making a jerk of yourself.

Each step I take does vibrate.
I feel blood course though my body for goodness sake!
Not a good sign I am very clear.
My burn-out is creeping near.

Sleep blessed sleep is sorely needed.
Clear my spirit, body, soul allow me to feed it.

Pain, confusion sets in,
you torment me; as if I was full of sin.

Burning, screaming, painful, final drain.
Oh my payment for life—is often one heck of a pain.

When I awake from my deep sound doze.
Stop my hands from shaking as I tweeze my brows.

Nothing could replace my complete self.
Post-polio stole that by itself.

Instead of crying; as it won't be of help.
I will take my repose; place my heart on the shelf.

I survived that terrible disease.
I am truly grateful I was rarely teased.

Honestly blessed to have had the joy to live.
I did; the only child to survive; now with much to give.

Thousands perished from that devil of a disease.
Now we bargain—allow me just a tad of ease.

Go to sleep ole body of mine.
Pray to wake in the eyes of Thine.

Energized, revitalized—ready to face another day.
Till you rear your ugly head—I swear you'll never make
me want for a day…

Our deal is clear—never forget.
Today you get me; tomorrow—don't place the bet.

As I will win; make no mistake!
You share my body; not own it for Heavens' sake!

Sleep blessed sleep is all I need.
The burnout will do to me as it does please.
As I awake the energy will pour;
My spirit, energy will overflow.

Post-polio has no cure, no recourse.
Tis like a boa constrictor, slithering rampant with no remorse.

Take it in stride.
Have plenty of pride.

Face the morrow.
No pity...no I'm sorry.

Night now my tired ole soul.
Tomorrow God willing you will reach your goal.

Smile
my life
sets my soul
totally completely
FREE.

Why?

Why are we full of greed?
Why does the world have famine?
Why do soldiers bleed?

Due to an un-necessary need.
Due to a lack of feed.
Due to weapons in wrong hands I feel.

Why do babies cry?
Why do parents die?
Why do we weep?

Due too hunger—a need for love.
Due too illness, war and plunder.
Due too pain, lost love, a child's plea-a need for sleep.

Why? Why?
Can we not try!
Let's work together—
We will be able to answer—

WHY?
Instead of cry,
Instead of die.
Instead of famine.

Because-
All mankind is worthy of love.

God's loving simple creation.
The child should weep not one more tear.
A soldier should be home with all who is dear.
Not one swollen belly due to hunger.
Loving arms to hold us stronger.

No more whys' or because.
Let's work together because of love.

The Critics Review

Kudos go out to you this day,
who's' poems I read with great delight.
Those of you, who trash the art,
should get on your knees to pray.
Forgive them Father for they not know;
the slash of their cruel tongues have a mighty blow.
If I am given the pleasure to read.
It is my ownership to review with care, not with speed.
I take up this gauntlet with a treasured pen.
Each poet deserves the best of my heart to send;
a message of hope, honestly, love and giving,
point out the positives of their works of art.
Never to bash their hearts delight.
Each poem is our own baby.
Not one for me to sit and degrade.
If ever I make the grade of a true poet.
I pray each one who reviews will know it.
Feel free to tell me if you got my message.
Feel free to tell me if you choose not to read.
I beg of you who—do not write.
To kindly take a hike…tonight.
So many of my peers have been bashed;
by your thoughtless tongues; are you smoking
hash?Every sonnet, poem or thought;
has great merit; whether you think it not.
Find the positives first I ask,
Be constructive; or just plain pass.

In The Name of Jesus I Pray—

For Brian and Alex

Dear Lord above Me,
I have a wee tiny prayer.
Two of your earthly angels,
Have been seriously burned this day.
Brian and Alex are just four years old.
I know not if; their stories are ready to be told.
The constant pain; now part their little life.
I beg of You my Lord; Guard them with your steady hand
one filled with the salve of your tender love.
Angels to surround them, these little ones'.
Place YOUR salve upon their burns.
Soothing the fiery pain.
Ease the hearts of Mommy and Daddy as well;
I have fear for them as well.
Dear Jesus,
Guide each one who comes near these babes.
Allow nothing to cause them any more pain.
With the touch from each doctor or nurse;
I beg of You—to be their Master.
Guide their touch so it is loving and gentle.
Offer them joy to be passed on to the children.
Allow nothing to stop your Mighty Hand;
In touching Brian and Alex as they lay so tiny in bed.

Please have your angels working over-time,
to tender special care, filled with your miracles, everywhere.
Love these wee ones; please make them strong enough to fight.
I pray to YOU;
please keep the family strong, always in your Hands tonight.
IN Jesus Name I beg of you;
Keep Brian and Alex strong; allow them to be healthy soon.
Blessed be the Name of Jesus; as you feel the families' pain.
Allow the parents to feel the strength of the Almighty;
As they wait for news of their babies this night.
MY prayer; to You Lord Almighty;
Allow Alex and Brian to be well very soon.
It is in your hands we will leave these two.
In our hearts we will pray to You. God grant Brian and Alex a respite from pain.
In their Mothers' arms soon again.
Blessed be the tiny child,
For without them we have not yet begun to learn.
Amen

God's Glorious Face

In memory of Brad Wentz (One Fallen Hero)

Iraq has yet taken another son,
away from those that love him.
Knowing he is in God's Mighty Hand;
blessed are those who knew him.

Why or who took away this fine young man;
we shall never fully understand.
In God's Glorious Face;
Brad does find his place.

In what we call; the Promise Land.
The throne Brad does sit upon,
Is golden; mighty grand,
befitting for this brave young man.

Loving family and friends left behind;
Iraq—did steal one special; so fine.
Brad; rest well, in your new found place.
Knowing you will always see God's Glorious Face.

Rest well my dear;
to all who hold you near.
Your spirit; never to be misplaced.
Knowing you are in "Your Rightful Place."

May God protect your family;
Your friends; each one in your unit.
I pray that soon there won't be;
Anyone from home left to Iraq.

Magic in the Air

Just listen—what do you hear?Open your eyes-what do
you see?
Birds chirping; children playing.
Wind blowing the cobwebs away.
I hear life all around.
New beginnings as spring surrounds.
Not just me; even the honeysuckle bees.
Nuzzling the joy of riches unfold.
Winter has past; with a mighty blast.
Rejoice in each day and night.
As the seasons come to pass.
I hear magic in the air.
Who it is for, I do not know; nor care.
Just rejoice; as it is there.
I see wonder everywhere!
From left to right—it is everywhere!
Look, feel, smile and celebrate.
We are here to share the tasty repast;
of seasons changing; ever so fast.
Enjoy life; as it is a brand new spring.
Soak up the sun as summer rolls in.
Stop, look and listen.
There is—magic in the air.

Their Way

Are you out to get me tonight?
Each poem I read gives such light.
I gaze upon the titles; then one jumps out to me.
Make my spirit soar with delight; take me closer to HE
He is the Lord Almighty.
He guides me to that place.
He makes me wonder who you are; to gaze upon your
face.
The power of the written word; is special to all of us.
Let's not be mean;
To ruin a dream.
As each one begins to float.
So you see;
The power you have can honestly sink a boat.
I search upon the titles written with such love.
They are your special babies;
I'll try to handle with kid gloves.
Take no offence to anything said;
I wouldn't deliberately say a negative word.Point out the
positives; they are written in gold.
Every poet needs to say it their way.

Thank you My Lord

My legacy in this life,
Is quietly settled down.
Not a day of strife,
Will catch them; too long with a frown.

Three charming smiles.
Three glorious pair of eyes.
Huge, warm, tender loving hearts; will walk the miles.
Much to my amazement, but never surprise.

One is tall, filled with brawn; topped off with a
permanent smile.
One is shorter; curly hair, with an oversized heart, full of
love.
The last one is tall, slender, and so sweet and tender; so
very young.
Three loves of my life; keep my spirit glowing.

Dear God; I cant thank you enough.
For the blessings you bestowed upon me.
Any pain or suffering I have ever had to endure.
The love from these three; you sent to comfort me.

Joys in my life,
Fearless forever,
knowing you my Lord;
have always carried my load.

My joys in life do number three.
The past; I'll not forget You.
The present; I thank You for the gift.
The future; which You will expose to me; when the time
is right.

Thank you my Savior,
Thank you for my loves.
Give thanks daily as; He is Our Lord.
Thank you for the joy; in seeing your sweet love.

Yes I have three; my legacy in life.
My son; my brave, brilliant, hardworking son.
My daughter, my smart, loving, joyous one.My little
granddaughter, sweet, funny, adorable, loving one.

How could I complain knowing,
Without Your love my Lord.
I would have nothing worth showing.
I would be totally bored.

Poems of Humor and of Love

Woes of my P.C.

First I try to connect
To the sweet internet
Woe and behold
My life is on hold.

My P.C. won't even start
I feel the pain into my heart.
How can my life carry on
If I can't type one single song?

Every port, plug and thingy,
has something in it. My ears are ringing!
Take it apart one by one;
I am going crazy…it won't even run.

Call a mechanic, plumber or technician;
I am on my way to daily confession.
I was a bad little puddy-tat; that I know
I used a potty-mouth word, now I must go.

Poor ole thing I counted on you.
Now my ole red-rimmed eyes are no longer blue.
You made me cry as I felt defeat.
I scream for help as all do sleep.

Crying won't help, as you well know.
Turn on the power-bar…look at her go!
Lookey, lookey I did it myself
My P.C. is working; no longer on the shelf.

Now a tweak here and there.
No longer am I pulling out my hair.
Type a ditty as I feel the need.Plant a laugh on the next persons' deed.

If you read this then you are IT!
A wee ditty about your P.C. will fit.
Send me a note to let me know.
I need to read now my P.C. does honestly go.

Bats and Bees Make Their Way

Here I am standing ready to fall,
my back barley holds up the wall.
Tire out puppy as one could be.
Dodging bats, hornets, and bees.

Hornets and wasps come for nowhere.
Darn dirty bat, entered the store unaware.
To the fruit he whisked straight away.
That cantaloupe and I certainly won't play.

Another long weekend tiss over I fear.
Thoughts of winter drive me batty with fear.
Mounds of snow will soon block my way.
Oh stay with me summer! I love to play!

Time escapes as each long weekend does pass.
Many laughs, pleasures, longing flirtatious passes.
Joys and spoils of summer pleasures.
Even bats and bees have moments to treasure.

Guys on the beach…hmmmmm my eyes do behold!
Gals do swoon; their eyes round with delight, often bold!
Eyeing up that the perfect one.
Soothing lotion on backs is reciprocal fun.

Alas we all must find time to eat.
Check out the stores…mmmm a wonderful retreat.
It pays to have the worlds' longest beach.
You may find this in-land water easy to reach.

Fresh eyes to behold, crimson sunsets.
Romance in the air just watch where you sit.
Not near the trees, nor the stores if you please.
That's where you find the bats and the bees.

Lay yourself down on our sandy beach with delight.
Savor each moment as UVA rays do light.
Dodge the bats with graceful movements.
Knowing Wasaga's finest has come once again this night.

Tourists, residents, one and all.
Take advantage of natures; delight; hear my call.
Pay heed to my warning; especially at night.
Keep way from the stores late at night…no dodging bats;
no fright.

Come one come all; tiss time to play.
Fifteen miles of wondrous sand.
Come ahead scope out this wondrous land.
Millions of people visit each year.

Keep ducking bees and bats.
Oh tourists; to us you are so dear; you fill our vats.
Water delicious, to drink and swim.
Night clubs do welcome you in.

Please consider it is safe to play.
Keep an eye on each other as you deem to play.
I say it over and over again.
Watch at night for stores do make hay.

As bats and bees to make their way.
By dawns early night.
They have all gone astray.
All that's left is radiant sunlight for you to play.

Come one come all we are delighted
To host you all; we are very excited.
One more long weekend is all we offer.
The pouting begins after; that I suffer.

Fraser to Fraser

Can you see it?
NO can you?
I can feel it!
Yucky-poo!

Help me please!
I've got to sneeze.Stop the flow
I gotta blow!

This tank is really blue,
Look at my hand…it is too.
Not my fault the thing just fell!
Into the bowl…like a wishing well.

Can you reach it?
It just can't stay!
The stick is stuck; oh yuck!
On your knees it is time to pray.

Get the seal,
Don't forget the bolts.
Try to feel,
Don't forget your notes.

How to do this dirty job?
Fraser and Fraser; begins to jog.
Get the parts, grab your tools.
On your knees you pair of fools.

Undo this!
Drain that!
Damn and piss!
Who forgot the hardhat?

In theory I am good.
In practice I suck.
That big blue tube
is really stuck!

We can do it you and me.
Together we will set this throne free.
Bolt by bolt, screw by screw,
What a job…everything is blue!

Piece by piece
Out it goes.
Smells delish,
Hold your nose.

There she be…
Set it free.
Can you get it?
Nope can you?

Need a snake?
No the hose will do.
Better off with a rake.
We could break it in two.

Bladder is running.
You gotta pee!
Stop your fuming,
We can see.

There it is that darn tube!
Get the hose; we'll float the joint.
Spray her baby! To the rim!
Oh! Look what's within.

Easy does it,
Out she goes.
Extra dry…
Hold your nose.

It's not funny!
Yes it is.
My eyes are runny.
What fun this is.

Once again, piece by piece,
we re-assemble the porcelain dish.
Tighten the bolts, turn the nuts.
We are better than plumbers; we are no klutz.

Water in the tank!
Water in the hold!
Course it works, let's give thanks.
Modesty, NEVER…as we are bold!

Congratulations are in order.
The secret no longer; a boarder.
Been evicted, kicked to the curb.
Now you may pee if you have the urge.

Sit gently, say a prayer.
What the heck, give a wee wiggle.
Relief is, the sweet smell; of fresh air.
Your home repair was quite a giggle.

Time to sign,
Fraser and Fraser—on the dotted line.
Tricks and fix—we can do.
To make you happy. Just to pee and poo.

Where Is My Pen

Has anyone seen my pen?
It was behind my ear.
I'm not sure; I thought it was my friend.
Tis hard to write without it near.
Had the right grip,
Fingers never slipped.
Oh well,
I'll blame the mistakes on the spell.
Like I even knew how
Spell check I'm not.
All I do is doodle and show,
Life's' joyous moments and forget-me-nots.
Looking high, looking low,
Where is my pen, do you know?
So I have lost it. The stores are full.
One that is balanced will write strong and true.
My poor pen is gone
But not the need.
To doodle a song
or scribble a ditty as I feel the need.

Tears of Laughter

Hey big man you think you so smart?
Momma has a trick in her heart.
Nibble on those crackers as you please.
I'll teach you well not too tease.
Shhhhh! To the cupboard I do go
crushing crackers very slow.
Wham! Bamm! All over your head.
Now I run—my life flashing ahead.
Tidy up you silly brat.That will teach you for yelling
scardey cat.
Little I may be.
Ha! The crackers down your shirt are free.
Oh! Your friend wants some of me too?
Easy does it. Tickle him blue.
Oh! The mess is a sorry sight.
What the heck I'll not clean tonight.
Thanks for the laughs, the exercise.
You bring tears of laughter to my eyes.

You Vant to Bite MY Neck!

You want to bite my neck!
I screech; while dashing about.
Your history; your past; I thought was someone's' last lament.
Brooms, glass, cast iron pans; all but my fear was broken; completely done.

With false courage I bellow, "Come any closer; I will clock you one!"
You roar at me, "I vant to bite your neck; my dear."
I quiver with fear; from your evil grin.
You lick your twisted lips; with a horrid smelling tongue.

Putrid feelings of hatefulness; is what I think of you.
"Come to my den of iniquity; I vant to taste your blood.
"Rare, sweet, sensual; tasty blood; I must indulge in a sip or two.
I won't wait; I must have you right here!"

Flap your wings; gone from my sight; fly away.
Be gone from my delicate neck.
My trusted bat and I shall never stray.
I have nothing left for you; just get out, go to heck.

You think you're strong!
Perhaps the odor of you.
I guarantee your judgment is wrong.
I'll not spare you one tiny drop or two.

Running, screaming; crying out in vain.
"You dirty; germ infested devil!
I have had more than enough pain.
You are nothing! Not worthy! Stay away from my vein!

Be gone! Go and have your sup;
Fly off to another's' neck this day.
One mighty smack will take you down; you'll never get
up.Dracula you're not; black flies yes; dead today!"

What Part of No Don't You Understand?

What part of NO don't you understand;
the beginning,
the middle,
or the end?

You waltz into my life,
thinking you still own me;
to do as you please.
Think again; you remind me of fleas.

What part of NO don't you understand;
the beginning,
the middle,
or the end?

I divorced you nineteen years ago;
For your misdeeds in our life,
The pain you did sow.
Is one of the reasons I am no longer you wife.

What part of NO don't you understand,
the beginning,
the middle,
or the end?

You toss a smirk on your face.
Tell me you want a wild night; with your ex-wife.
Bold and brassy you will always be;
Now the cake on your face;
is as plain as can be.

What part of NO don't you understand,
the beginning,
the middle,
or the end?

Only two things do we have left in common;
You ignore them; so what is your problem?
Oh I see another for the road.
Take the whole case while it's still cold.Just be gone as
you leave me ice-cold.

What part of NO don't you understand,
the beginning,
the middle,
or the end?

Always a loser never a doubt,
Always a drunkard; forever a lout.
Forever a stranger to those you should see.
Your beautiful children,
Created by you and me.

What part of NO don't you understand,
the beginning,
the middle,
or the end?

Leave me out of your miserable life!
Never forget I am no longer your wife!
Shake yourself up and settle down.
Oh; I forgot you would rather drown.
Your own self pity; is always around.

What part of No don't you understand,
the beginning,
the middle,
or the end?

So now I will tell you plain and clear.
Be gone from my sight;
I don't need you near.
If it wasn't for the kids; I would have locked you out.
Passed you by as your reach for yet another stout.

No I won't ask again what you don't understand.
Just stay away;
Or you will rue the day.
To me you no longer linger; you don't symbolize a man.
Just a slight shadow with still; a beer in his hand.

Pancake Bum

I am but one silly one;
Getting to old for me and my knees.
All I needed to do;
Was start the lawnmower indeed.

Instead you gave me grief;
You stubborn ole thing.
When the boss gets home tonight, your cord will be
given; one mighty reef.
That's when I'll begin to sing.

All I wanted of you, you miserable piece of junk!
Was to mow and clean the yard so nice; you aged, old
piece of grief.
So my son does tell me; that I am too small,
To pull the cord with all my strength; not land flat on my
butt; near the wall.

Tis not a pretty site; of that I am quite clear.
All of five foot four;
My butt smacked; flat to the wall.
It hurt more than my dignity; I hope you daren't see.

I bruised more than my flat little butt;
I think I cracked the wall.
So now my giant son come home.
Flex those biceps; your full of brawn.

Pull that darn cord, cut the grass;
Or I promise you—more than a slightly bruised ass.
Oh that smirk I can see already glowing your face.
As you unload your brand new mower; to groom the grass; as you race.

No dinner for you again tonight.
You overgrown child of mine.
The lawn has need of your care this night.
Or I will hire a competitor; of thine.

That will wipe the smirk off your face.
As I rub my tush indeed.
To need to pay Fitzy for doing your place.
I will laugh and run with glee!

I quit forever my dear son,
Pulling weeds is fun.
Least it gets me out of the house;
Plus; I know—I won't land on my pancake bum.

Take the Shot—

I Am Rid of Migraine

Pain does thunder through my head.
Another migraine for sure I dread.
Thank heavens for Doctor Sloan with his mighty shot.
Just one here, another there, on and on;
Soon the migraines will be gone.
No need any longer to crawl into my darkened room;
fighting pain; wracking my body and brain.
Tick tock; let's try nerve block.
I am game for anything;
Your best shots I will take All!
My life had been full of hellish pain;
With so much lost and nothing gained.
Now I am free of that paralyzing pain.
Thank heavens; for those shots to my head.
I needn't hide under the covers, filled with dread.
Each day a blessing;
Pain free to be sure.
Just a wee pinch here and there;
I honestly don't care.
Bring them on,
I'll take the lot!
Suffering for forty years;
I have no fears.
Nerve block today;
Is safe to say;

Least on each morrow,
I will be ready to play with absolutely no sorrow.
Bring them on each mighty shot.
I gladly take the lot!
I feel renewed;
Ready, willing and able,
To go forth; enjoy each and every day.
My final words I would have to say;
Thanks to Dr. Sloan; with is mighty shot.
He is a man I would forget me not.
As migraine is a long past pain.

Tis All MY Fault

Tis gone I am afraid,
Now my time to lament.Six long weeks I waited for my friend;
Only to fine it bent.
Who was mighty demon? It wasn't given up for Lent.
Who dared to stress me out!
Gulp; could have been me I suppose.
As I wasn't very patient.
So now I sit in my own tears.
Eyes red-rimmed for sure; my keyboard is dead.
Perhaps I pass on the blame to the ghosts of my typing mistakes.
Perhaps I will pass it on to the hours I spend in the lake.
No I mustn't blame anyone; tis my own foolish deed.
Not says the devil in me; t'was Bell Canada indeed.
If they hadn't been out on strike, yet again I'd say.
My darling sweet computer would never have caved in on me that day.
How was I to know they would make me wait for years?
Yes to you it was six little weeks,
To me; it feels like years.
Write things out in longhand!
My son you really must be out of your mind.
My poor ole hand are bent and twisted,
The pen I will hold no more.
Oh you laugh you overgrown devil!
Look out you may feel the broom on your behind.
NO! I won't take the broom for a ride.

Be gone from me; I need to think of what I need to try.
Would you rather see me wither up and cry?
Off you go and I mean today; no don't call me a sucky witch.
I have the right to whine, witch and chew.
Find Mommy a new keyboard please?
One that is straight, strong, will love my touch; all brand new.
One that has a warrantee to.
I'll suck up the blame; I know it's my fault!
I should have asked for help.
Waiting six long weeks did let me putter instead.
I just chose to try to put together, by myself.
So I am stubborn; just like my Mother.
Could be worse I could be like Dad,
On second thought; if I were like Dad,
My bottom lip wouldn't be pouting mad.
As he would have worked diligently, to put each plug in port.
Gleefully saying at the end.
No Motherboard plug did I bend!

Molly Maid

As I awoke this morning;
many thoughts running through my head.
I couldn't help but yawning.
As I dust the cobwebs; away from the beds.
Some call me Molly Maid;
I take no offence.
As I certainly find it warming;
A compliment instead.
No fuzzy dust balls gather;
Just give me one tiny chance.
I'll crank the tunes; dance around;
The swifter in my hand.
Being tidy isn't hard for me;
Military raised and bred.
Bring on the daily inspection;
No dust balls; will mess with my head.
They make me sneeze,
Sometimes wheeze;
Please be not; in my way.
For if you are, I'll make you grin.
Dusting high and low; is not a deadly sin.
I know you find it funny;
Watching me reaching for one little dust filled space.
Listen to my warning! Wipe that smirk off your face.
Don't worry about the climbing.
My step stool is almost; tall enough.
Now you call me a midget; keep telling me not to fall.
If only I were taller;
That stool I wouldn't need.

I would rock the tunes much louder.
Having fun while I do my deed.
Change the music; crank it up.
While I shimmy and shake.
If all are good; you may have a gift.
Of your birthday cake instead.
Now you take back;
The Molly Maid crack.
You know I do not care.
We are rid of the germs; with time to spare.
Now it's time to have my shower, wash away the grime.
Don't let out my secret; as you know I'll clean quite happily any ole time.

The Nasty Bug

Would that I could score one to ten,
Today would have been a minus twenty.
All I did was lay about, cough, and sneeze.
My nose is mighty red.
If only it was Christmas time;
I would be leading Santa's' sled.
This nasty bug is going round.
I fear is will not end.
Oh well; says' I.
I will not die from this wee cold in my head.
On the morrow it should ease;
That certainly would be a pleasure.
Like finding the map along the way;
To fleece the golden treasure.
So back to bed I must scurry.
First wipe down the germs.
Clorox wipes do the job;
alright; they clean up in a hurry.
Goodnight to you one and all;
I pray you do not a victim fall.
To this lousy cold or virus.
I wouldn't wish upon a mouse.

Time for Bed

Ok little one it is time to go to bed.
I think not say I; to my man-child instead.
You are younger than I and need your rest
So off you go instead.
Grinning from ear to ear; he silent rubs his hands.
Knowing a deep, deep sleep will soon be knocking me
flat.
Oh no I am not stubborn;
Does the old oak tree bend?
I am just not sleepy;
I am in need of my pen.
I write with pleasure;
Sometimes show and tell.
That's when I am not sleepy.
Or post polio rears its' head.
Shall we wake the birds to sing?
A lullaby for us?
I think the neighbors would have a say,
Some might even cuss.
Now I'll go and view the stars,
Giant as can be.
Perhaps I'll pick a few,
Some for me and the rest for you.
See how I avoid my bed.
'Tis comfy to be sure.
I just don't want to miss the night.
As during the day, 'tis very hard to see.

Poetic Un-license

Would that I could;
Take back the time.
After reading your comments,
About poems of mine.
I feel like stink!
Not from a hockey rink.
A total dink for not reading the line.
One that should have given you all you deserved.
The dropping of the gavel. My mistake.
Please forgive me I am but a fool.
Never again do I miss the gavel.
My spirit had been totally unraveled.
For that to all I have insulted.
Please forgive my poetic un-license.

Sold but Not to Be Forgotten

Pack up the boxes here I go,
Moving slowly to where I do not know.
This ole body is feeling slow.
Never let it be said feeling low.
My home was sold without anyone knowing;
Just the old and new owners; who are now glowing.
A fancy dollar…was made on the sale.
A vacation from stress shall make my spirit sail.
One month at the resort; I remember so well.
Sit back, relax, and do not fail!
Keep the pen and paper handy. To me it is addictive like chocolate candy.
Just one little month and my new abode will be ready.
The internet installed; with plenty of work ready.
Please be advised. I will re-appear with a vengeance.Ready to pay homage to all that is present.
I pack the last box with a smile on my face.
Knowing the joys of a new found place.

The Jokester Strikes

Bill my son, dream; make all of your dreams come alive.
Go for it!

Are you toying with me yet again?
Playing it safe are we…bringing your friend?
You can't be teasing; tell me the truth!
Don't toss it off as you would a worn out tooth.
You sold your racecar! I can't take it all in.
She was your baby; all shiny; just a trace of blue.
Oh my son; you are a terrible tease; tell me true.
Keep trying and trying to ruffle my feathers.
I know. You always said," I aim to please."
A jokester I have raised.
God bless him…he is a fine young man.
Sometimes I think he should have felt the bottom of my
hand.
No…that wouldn't be me.
I raised him to set his spirit free.

Poems of Love

Soon

(Looking Towards Tomorrow)

Soon the sun will shine.
Soon I will be reborn.
To see my special place; with morning sun.
Sunlight glistening on still waters.
Returning to my roots makes me feel; strong.
Glorious faces of friends; sorely missed.
Watching the sunset, from my special place.
Embrace the change…it will be good for me.
Freedom to run about: seeking laughter,
Soon winter will have past.
Soon the misfortunes of the past
Shall be gone, leaving a life reborn.
Away and awake I will explore the dawning of a new life.
Taking hold with all I may embrace.
Once again I shuffle on.
Looking for the day to begin at dawn
soon life will feel like a newborn babes'.
Soon…meaning; will come to my joyous place.

The Sunrise of Heaven's Gates

To you who see the good side of life.

Wake up sleepy heads.
Get up and get out of bed.
Tis a quarter past five make no mistake.
I need to see the sunrise of Heavens' Gate.Not a creature
is stirring round this town so far.
Birds still nesting their downy heads.
Hurry up or you will miss yet another sunrise!
Ahhhh! Here it comes; slow but delightful.
The sky is beginning to ribbon with blue.
I see clouds dancing wildly through the sky.
The wind will soon blow the cobwebs away.
Hear the whistle blowing;
it must be six-fifteen.
Lights are coming on; in this sleepy lil' town.
I hear the cats and dogs beginning to scramble.
Finding their way home after a night on their own.
The morning sun does begin to rise.
Ribbons of red streak through the sky.
I see purple with gray clouds drifting on by.
They can't upset the sunrise of Heaven's Gate.
A little ole man comes out of his house.
Looking, searching to find his paper.
Take a moment as he did do.
Look to the sky; a vision of perfection you may ever see.
Why is that you ask of me?
To see the sunlight dancing over the Bay of Quinty.
Dancing on the water with diamonds a plenty.

Trains whistle by; no stop they did make.
People beginning to shower and stumble.
Off to work or play;
Taking for granted this glorious day.
I wake each morn with a smile on my face.
Knowing without a doubt I'll see the sunrise of Heavens'
Gate.
Her beauty is never ever the same.
Good thing as for tomorrow I will be waiting.
Turn on the coffee,
Wash away the sleep;
be prepared for one more peek.
Always in awe; of God's mighty hand.
With the sunrise of Heaven's Gate.

Capture Your Dreams

To My Son...Never Look Back

Mom, I want to go fast;
says her son with a grin.
Shrugging her shoulders. So my son; go fast.
Get your car; find the track; watch your skin.

Knuckles will bruise;
Like the sheet metal you lose.
As you mend your car;
From one tiny kiss.

Not on the lips you silly man.
The wall...
First night out...you smiled ear to ear.
Placing sixth!

Wow...what a fix!
Palpitations from me...Not!
You have the need, feel and the nerve.
Follow your dreams.

As I have begged you to do.
Finally you have...I totally rejoice.
Go fast my son.
Keep in mind...one day you will be number one!

I never want you to have a regret,
in not going after your dreams...and yes your Vette.
You make me proud;
Hearing cheers from the crowd .Go! Number thirteen!...so
loud.

Bill Laughlin; number thirteen; new to the game.
Rookie you are,
Only in…
That…hot looking racecar.

You dig in and work hard.
You give more than any man.
It's your time to play;
So take the car…catch the rush!

'I love your smile…your glowing blush.
Go fast as you feel.
Take the pack as you need.
Pick them off; like tiny seeds.

Not a traffic cop around; No tickets to pay.
Go fast young man.
Get out and play.

Reach out; capture your hearts delight.
In you; I have such love;
my pride definitely wins the race;
it was there…even; before I saw your face.

Now go out there with a smile on your face.
Take the checkered flag and my heart with every race.
I won't cower; when the cars' not right.
That's racing…there will be another night.

I adore your determination.
To…"Just suck it up!"
Go! Go! Number thirteen.
Reach out…Capture Your Dreams.

Strong, Honest and Free

To My Children and Granddaughter…With Love and Respect

My loves in life are numbered three.
Bill, Beth and Shaughnessy.
Two of my loves are all now grown;
The youngest one; has a daughter of her own.
I have no fears of their hearts content.
Their feet are planted firmly in cement.
Every day has gathered emotions…
Honestly some have…unfurled commotions.
Let hem scrap with words alone.
In a matter of minutes you will hear the phone…
I love you no matter what; will be spoken aloud.
We may differ constantly but that is allowed.
You were raised to respect each other;
Thank God for a Mother and Father.
Now the wee one will face life in a different path.
A new generation of troubles may get in her way.
Shaughnessy; be strong…grin away;
Tell them to get out of your way.
Go forth my children. With or without me.
I raised you to be strong, honest and free.
I thank God for your place in my life.
I hope…each day is filled with a taste of delight.

When I Use to Fit

Tell me about the days when I use to fit.
In the days of old when all was young.
Life had meaning; so different from now.
A reason to wake up...boogie around.
Getting kids off to school with happy sounds.
Now half a century plus has past.
The needs dreams and desires fading fast.
Yes...still needed; but on a slow moving pace.
Play with my grandchild with occasions of bliss.
Waiting for the weekend; for her angelic kiss.
Not a daily fix do I receive any longer.
The miles too many; for a morning smooch.
Who changed the rules of life past fifty?
Not I for sure; just Father Time.
Now I look in the mirror and say.
Someone tell me the rule each passing day.
I love my man, his kids and grandson.
I pray someday we will be as one.
Then life again will be a perfect fit.

Are You My Friend?

For Shaughnessy from Nanna

Have you managed to catch the glow?
Look around…see the child;
She makes you tingle; her spirit surrounds.
Laughing at nothing; being her happy self.
That's my little one; Shaughnessy.
Happy to breathe; life's' happy sounds.
Just a hug; kiss or nudge;
perhaps a piece of Poppas' fudge.
"Momma," she says with a devilish grin,
"School today?" with a charming grin.
Her Mommas' angel she will always be; loved to bits.
"Are you my friend?" she will ask.
"Yes baby." we say." I am your friend."
Smother you with kisses; as she goes off to school.
Her smile is delightful; can you catch her glow?
That's my girl, her Mommas' pearl.
Smile as she and your spirit will be free.

Touch

Make me wish you were mine.
Your touch; though gentle was scorching hot.
Our bodies tangled; my hands in thine.
You touched my heart when you said forget me not.

I felt completed as you kissed me senseless.
Your hands touched mine; our spirits connected.
Was it a dream; where were my defenses?
No dream there as you were real; just unexpected.

Curley hair, big blue eyes;
a love of life;
Peaceful thoughts; no good-byes.
How I wish I was your wife.

The Face I Do Not See

Should I fall asleep tonight,
Would you be my safety net?
Dare I drift off to nod,
Please enter; show me your wondrous way.
Your face is still a mystery;
One I have yet to see.
Thoughts are scorching through my soul,
Your name, I don't you know?
I have mirrored with fascination as you creep into my
dreams.
With a touch so profound,
I fall to the ground,
Joined as one,
Mind, body, heart, spirit and soul.
Whisper words of wisdom; as you always do to me.
Tis my imagination; bringing your face nearer to see.
No it isn't the shelter from the stormy night.
That brings us close together each and every night.
It may well be my fantasy, one of pure delight…
My subconscious telling me;
That all this will be right.
Don't fight what you can't see. Your face well hidden for
sure.
I know my spirit sound; always running free.
Making the message clear.
Keep one foot on the ground.
Watch where you go indeed.

It is my own subconscious; talking me round;
Faceless, fearless; without any dread.
So now I will be off to my slumber
Perhaps I will saw logs instead.
Perhaps the face I do not see;
Is my own; having a serious talk with me.

My Precious Boo

To Beth, My darling daughter; you fight for everything in life.

Boo; I love you as if you didn't know.
You picked me up when I was down.
Even when I drove you nuts you never let it show.
Roll me over in my lowly bed;
you fed me with a spoon.
Taught me how to walk.
Weeks later when I could finally leave the room.
You are a tad defiant;
told a doctor where to go!
When he shrugged his shoulders;
said "Hell just put her in a home!"
You carried me to and from the ladies room non-stop.
Patience is your virtue my love.
You never once gave up!
You know I am very grateful for all the magic you show
Those strong healing hands did me well;
As I finally took a step.
Into your chest I fell.
God bless you and Shaughnessy,
You gals have had it mighty tough.
Now I am a walking tiger;
Give me the little one; go have some fun yourself.
You deserve a bouquet of roses;
I know you would toss them out.
No flowers for you just a night or two free.
We have never given; love a doubt.

Letter to My Father

To my mentor, The man who taught me how to be just ME. My late Father.

Hi Pops,
My precious bald eagle.
I have missed you so much while you are away.

You woke me up again last night;
In my dreams of you.

I know it has been a very long time,
Since you went to Heaven.

Your sweet gentle smile; still lights up my life.
Although you left so many years ago.

This morning was very tough indeed.
As I realized; you were just five years older than I.

When God chose your name for Heaven.
We talked about when, it would be time.

To make our way up the stairs;
Leaving all eight of us; must have given you a few fears.

You were ready to go home; you told me.
I knew exactly what You meant.

You planned out all of the details;
as I sat at the end of your hospital bed.

To finally lay your body down.
You told me not to worry; as a halo had been found.

I know for certain you are with me.
You couldn't ever stray.

Wise man; my Daddy, my mentor,
You're still my everything.

You taught me right from wrong;
You made me tie my shoes.

Most of all my dearest Dad;
I learned how to LOVE from YOU.

So now you are in; God's loving home.
Mom is at your side.

I hear the chairs are golden,
the angels' voices singing.

God's sweet expression,
as He took you aside.

You my son, I have chosen;
to guide your family from here.

See the sweet expressions;
On the face that holds you dear.

Her time is not coming yet,
The pain she will overcome.

The memories of your sweet, sweet face.
I shall never ever erase.

Rest now dear Daddy;
You put up a valiant fight.

I heard St. Peter calling;
Lawrence, please come home tonight.

I go about my daily life.
I have for many years.

Not a single day goes by.
I know you are standing closely by.

Thank you for the memories.
Thank you for the love.

Thank you for instilling in me.
My love for all and God.

Now I close this letter,
I'll mail it with the angels once again tonight.

I will love you forever;
Miss your laughter of delight.

Tons of love; dear Pops.
Your loving daughter.
Mary

How Much Do You Love Me?

To My Darling Shaughnessy; who figured out what infinity means.

Now ease your head my baby;
Lay it right next to me.
Let me feel your shallow breathing;
AS I am so proud of you.
I need to see you sleep.

Let me gently stroke your face as you nod off.
Let me touch those puckered lips.
Don't wake too soon; my darling.
You're a treasure; my pleasure;
I love to watch you sleep.

Many, many years I wished for;
you my love, just your heart, body and soul.
Too many dreams I had;
Praying you not to be bold.
Half a century I begged for you.

For years I have begged for you, one tiny little kiss.
Now God and all the angels will laugh.
Your precious hand I hold.
When you say how much you love me?
It is with pure hearts' delight.

How much do you love me?
I whisper in your ear; with a stolen, soft butterfly kiss.
Your tiny hands slowly stretch.
Way up high you see.
Infinity and beyond is not big enough.

How much then do you love me?
I whisper into her ear once more.
Her fingers point all around; wiggling left and right.
To the stars and the sun right back to this earth.
To God's House in Heaven; I love you that much.
Pleasure shoots right through me;
each time she snuggles close.
"Nanna," she quietly asks "How much do you love me?"
Oh my darling angel; I love you from head to toe.
Nanna loves her little Doll; with all her heart and soul.

To infinity and beyond isn't anywhere near enough;
My love for you keeps growing.
Your smile; big hearted; even when sleep is coming your
way.
"You need to thank the angels for keeping you safe".
"Yes my little Doll" I whisper right back.

Point my own fingers high and say to the Angels and
God's house.
That much and for every day I have loved you with all
my heart.
You are a smart one; to have found where Heaven is.
Know what else I know; she giggles with delight.
I know we can talk to God any old time we want.

Just find your star. In the Heavens.
Settle in; Talk to God each night.
Don't forget to thank God for letting this world be here
for you.
Talk to your angels my sweet one.
They know of what you mean; you may even whisper;
your voice will travel on a moonbeam.

Starry Nights

For all who would rather stargaze than sleep.

This night is calm, nary a cloud in the sky,
I watch, look and listen to glorious night sounds.
Thoughts drift furiously through my head, I should be
sleepy but don't know why.
Faster than pixie dust floating around;
I discover the reason I have yet to lay down.
Mysterious stars, shoot though the sky;
My wish—is never be angry—never to frown.
The brilliance above me shines ever so bright.
Who needs sleep; when stars are dancing tonight.
Pick out your favorite, I dare you!
Mine is the galaxy; joyously tumbling all around.
Not twinkle, twinkle, tiny star.
Giant globes; shining brilliant for all of us to view.Careful
how you turn your head.
Starry nights; could keep you from bed.
I love stargazing each and every night.
They bring me a jolt of pure delight.

My Mother's Gilded Chair

In loving memory of my Mother.

"Soon my daughter I am going away."
Came my Mother's voice; for the first time in days.
"Mom, may I go with you when you go."
"Not now my darling. Tis not your time you know."

Those first words spoken in many a day
as my sweet tiny Mother had been in a coma for days.
"I have seen a glimpse of this place
OH how wonderful; a glorious space."

"Momma will I ever see you again?"
Were the only words I could whisper in pain.
"Yes, my Mary; you will see me once more
Your golden chair is standing close to all you adore."

"Momma" I cry out; to keep her speaking
trying to hold on just a little longer
"Take me with you please!" I begged.
"NO my baby—my journey is on its last leg.

"I caught a glimpse of Heaven today,"
My darling mother did quietly say.
"All of the Angels are gathered around.
What wondrous look of joy on everyone's face; smiles
abound.

"Your Gilded chair stands ready for each of you
Close to God; surrounded with lasting eternal love.
Whenever you need me or feel any strife.
Look to the stars, I will be on the right,

"Singing from Heaven;
Where His glory shines.
Is the magical wonder of Heaven; I'm no longer in pain.
Be patient, love one another, don't let anyone fight, never
forget to have prayed.
"Your Guardian Angel will always be there;
As will all; who have gone home before me that care…"
Hazel eyes slowly looked up; a sweet secret smile; upon
her face.
During the terrifying time near my Mothers' demise; we
wouldn't leave her space.

Many private moments my Mother had,
with her angels; always happy never sad.
Joy formed a halo round Mom's sweet head.
We knew the presence of Angels and God s' Glorious Face.

Had come to fill our spirit with joy; to ease our own pain.
By taking my mother Home to stay.
Not a word was spoken as she took her last breath.
We knew by then; she had been born brand new.

Our Father in Heaven has a mighty hold,
Bestows upon us; pleasures to behold.
Allows us the freedom to mourn as we need.
He fills our spirit with his spirit you see.

Never walk alone; down any path,
Our Lord is the Master, He does the math.
When our time comes; the Gilded golden chair awaits.
As we reach the beauty of Heaven's Gate.

Wish her back; I cannot.
Miss her; absolutely have no doubt.
Pray to Mom and Dad each night.
I ask them to help, God with all mans' strife.

I am waiting for my day to come.
Not for many a year plus one.
Then I shall see as the angels do.
The love of mankind; of me and you.

Blessed be the angels sing.
Blessed be the Gilded chairs.
Blessed be my parents as well.
Blessed be God; the CREATOR of us all.

Job Well Done

To David, Jason and Patti, and their son Porter

Lay your head down...let me ease your heart.
Today will soon be tomorrow,
Fresh clear and bright;
That is the passing of day into night.

All that makes your heartache;
God's gentle hands will take.
Open yourself to His mighty ways
He is the Master of our days.

The time has come to say goodbye.
Forever; as time won't stop.
Your place is sitting; next to Him.
As you finally rest in peace.

Look down and smile...
As you say with your tiny grin;
Hey...I did it. I win!
Strong, bright, loving secrets delight.

In a Mothers' love;
Sent on the wings of a dove.
Knowing her legacy of life goes on;
Come Christmas; her grandchild will be here.

When it snows,
They are kisses from Grandma.
When it rains;
She is missing your touch.

As the sun shines;
She is caressing your skin.
Rest now dear Heather.
Your job was well done!

Drops of Rain

For My Late Parents

I felt your laughter,
as lightening lit up the sky.
Shared a moment with new friends.
Such a secure feeling.The wind and rain,
Whipping round my home,
Washing away the grime.
From the outside; cleansing within.
Wild winds blew drops of rain,
Like kisses from Heaven.
I felt loved from Above.
Guide me well,
Keep me strong,
Make me laugh,
Let me be just be ME.
A creature; the best of both of you.
Your strength,
Your stamina,
Mostly reminds me life is precious…
To grab it; with an open heart and hand.
See…
Your lessons in life,
haven't been wasted;
by your passing,
from this world to the next.

Hello Little Bump

To my daughter and grandchild (part of my Sanity…Journal)

Hello little bump,
Yes I know you are there.
Soon; you will give a thump.
Looking for something to wear.

Take your time, there is no rush.
Warm in your sacred womb.
You will rock, roll, kick and push.
Trying to make room.

Trust me there will be time,
To make your presence known.
Before we know it you will be here.
With candles to be blown.

We will celebrate the moment of your birth.
Your Mom will be excited.I MAY come down to earth.
Take your time…easy does it.

The world is big,
It can be scary…
Not to worry,
Your Mom will always be there.

From the Bump to Mommy

(with help)
*Two of my shining stars. Liz, my daughter and Shaughnessy,
my precious granddaughter.*

Hi Mom,
I just thought I would say hi.
You can't hear me and I know why.
I'm too small,
Not ready yet.
Curled in a ball.
Waiting to stretch.
In a few weeks,
You will feel me tickle,
From within;
I may even ask for a pickle.
Please Mommy take good care.
Brush your teeth, get plenty of rest.
As I grow…
Your body will definitely stretch.
Yes, my arm here, under your ribs.
How about a bum on your hip?
I have hic-cups, make no mistake.
I may even suck my thumb.
You won't know yet,
Cause Nanna won't tell.
She is writing this for me…
Remember I am too small.
Just to tell you.
I will love you with my all.
Night, night Mommy.
All my love.
From the Bump.

Goodnight Sweet Boo

To my daughter Liz

What lays nestled upon my bed?
Waiting for stories to be read.
My small tiny kitten...you see;
She is very real to me.
The days go rapidly by; as time flies.
Soon will be the time,
to finally lay my head to rest.
One more book to read,
One more mouth to feed.
A snuggle or cuddle.
The scent of your skin to breathe in.
My kitten is real.
My cultured pearl.
Created from love.
God's gift from above.
Tiny angelic and peaceful she lays.
Waiting for the last whispered words of the day.
Sleep well my little kitten.
Purr into the night, with sweet dreams.
My kitten; is you; my own sweet Boo.

Boots

My pretty little Purr…How I miss your rumble.

When you hear a sound,
Off you go in leaps and bounds.
You hide in a safe dark place.
Curled up with a sweet contented face.

Black and white,
No gray in you.
Little white stockings,
Are boots on you.

My pretty little Purr,
Out you come when we're alone.
Your voice does rumble,
Sure steps never stumble.

Unlike me, Yet so much alike.
Both are cats.
You of one kind, me the other.

I pet you,
You soothe me.
Forever I will care for you.
Your love is totally free.

My sweet little girl,
Gave you to me.
She is my treasured pearl.
God's Grace gave her to me.

Contemplate No More

Don…I love you more than you will ever know.

Today I sit and contemplate.
The days ahead are ours to debate.

Do I shower the world with love and compassion?
Or make my way with worldly passion.

Lead with my heart; my spirit does say.
For all tomorrows bring joys into play.

Some I see…others I miss.
A dreaded thought to have missed a kiss.

Our children have grown and fled the nest.
In search of their own; to make it the best.

My dear heart is my lifeline…he keeps me sound.
We have each other to carry us through; to keep my feet
on solid ground.

Contemplate no more; can you see my smile.
Step closer; take my hand, lets' walk together one more
tiny mile.

Bond as no other: love as hard as you can.
Always remember…Don you were meant to be my man.

One Two Three

Time is slipping slowly away;
Today I have shaken the cobwebs at play.
Get yourself up; out of this dump.
Only I can dig from under; this slump.
The world is there; why aren't I?
My quiet place I need to be...
I cannot see.
So get off your butt! Open your eyes!
Count your blessings.
One, Two, Three.
I have a pulse; also a brain.
Get off your butt...don't miss the train.
My gift of life has given me many values.
Wake up! Get up! Fight back!
Don't let the dreaded spiders win!
You know life is as sweet as candy.
Time to take yet another bite.
Wake up; give it one hell of a fight.
I am strong; been there before; won't cave in!
Post polio doesn't have a chance to win.
Be strong, shake it off.
Now!
One, two, three.

Dear Ol' Adopted Dad

To Rog with love for always keeping me sane.

You are always there to make me smile.
From miles apart you share your heart.
When I am troubled you sense my fear.
Magically, you appear.
Your unconditional love makes the day just right.
Your prayers at night keep me safe and tight.
You and Momma are always there,
Allowing me my troubles to share.
We rejoice together in all that's good.
Sharing laughs makes life a sweet gain.
My Dear Ole' Adopted Dad,
I pray your life never to be sad.Each night the stars are
yours and mine.
I pray for you and all of mankind.
The day we met was a good connect.
Thank you, Dear Ole Adopted Dad.
For making me your adopted daughter.
Remember who loves you D.O.A.D.
Your bambino, your A.D.,
Is so very glad.

Yes...I Believe It Is True

To my son Bill...You never cease to amaze me...

I requested your presence in my life.
Child of mine, now you are grown.
A man you have become;
More than I had imagined,
On the eve of your birth.
I prayed you be tall,
I prayed you to be strong.
I begged you be a clear thinker.
Yes...my prayers came true.
You make me proud...in all you do.
You have ability;
To make all around you laugh.
Shield your own; from much pain.
Face down life's' fears;
With your incredible ability to work hard.
Life's' challenges are faced with honor,
As they are placed in your path.
Go with your dreams.
Be realistic...
With your expectations of others.
Hold your family with open arms.
Smile sweet son,
That secret, special smile of yours.
You are full of charms.
All I prayed for; in your life my son,
I believe it is true.

This last poem is in this book twice. It is
dedicated to all those that read my hearts
sweet thoughts.
I thank you for reading them.
Remember that no matter what else you
do in this life.
Always "Just Be You" and
you will be loved for "You."

Just Be You... But Take Notes.

"To all those who teach, by allowing us to read."

So many creative minds out here;
could put you in a block.
An opinion, review or tear shed for someone there.
Could make me take a walk.

I have read such beauty,
Cried for hours;
as I read the tearful words, heart tugging pleas.
Of war, starvation, depravation plus the lack of men in
powers.

Oh I am no spineless chicken here,
Just a newbie in this forum.
Read my words...with thoughtful eyes
There is a message in subtle disguise.

Your gifts of words go with value and trust;
Flower it up...
That's' not me...
For if did. It would be a bust.

Whispering words of willow trees,

That's not me you see.
I write from my heart...
Straight out and true.
Honest, loving, gentle, truthful to be sure.

The humbleness of reading your words;
Brings me to my knees.
I feel joy; remorse; pity; resounding memories record;
As I lay blue eyes upon this screen; my heart held in my
hand.

You captured my essence of living; you showered my life
with joy;
you have dropped me to my knees with forgiving.
This forum is not a toy.

WE write for many reasons;
Of which I know a few.
Once a change of seasons.
Now it is…to grow anew.

To be re-born with wisdom
isn't…what all do have.
To be born with a cherished mind.
Is a gift from God above.

Savor each word…spice it up.
Learn from your mentors.
Take notes…write it up!
NEVER defer from the real YOU!
Or you will have dandelions for your sup.

Bio

Mary Winnifred Fraser

Born in Whitehorse, Yukon, Northwest Territories, Tues. August 12, 1952.

I have always had a dream deep within my soul to one day publish a book of poetry or children's stories.

At the age of seven I had a dream that I was a writer; ever since that night I still dream that dream.

I have had many blessings in my life; with great rewards. (My family and grandchild)

I had yet one small regret.

That I hadn't achieved my one goal to become a writer.

I love to sit to the computer and just let my spirit take over and feel the rhythm of the keys dancing with words across the page.

Each and every poem I write comes straight from my heart.

Yes, I have been blessed a time or two in my writing moments to have someone read one of my poems and tell me that it made them feel better, soft smiles appear, made them laugh, get all misty-eyed or connect with the pictures they see in their own mind.

To be able to touch a heart with the written word is a blessing to be sure.

I honestly can say that I wake thinking of writing and won't sleep period; if I have a wee thought running around in my head. I have to write it out!

I feel my life has been touched in a very special way through poetry.

My dear Poet-Friend.

Bruce

God Bless You
and yours
always

Lot of Love

Mary Fraser

Printed in the United States
43218LVS00002B/1-60